Summary of

The Advantage

by Patrick Lencioni

Instaread

Instaread on The Advantage by Patrick Lencioni

Please Note

This is a key takeaways and analysis.

Copyright © 2015 by Instaread. All rights reserved worldwide. No part of this publication may be reproduced or transmitted in any form without the prior written consent of the publisher.

Limit of Liability/Disclaimer of Warranty: The publisher and author make no representations or warranties with respect to the accuracy or completeness of these contents and disclaim all warranties such as warranties of fitness for a particular purpose. The author or publisher is not liable for any damages whatsoever. The fact that an individual or organization is referred to in this document as a citation or source of information does not imply that the author or publisher endorses the information that the individual or organization provided. This concise summary is unofficial and is not authorized, approved, licensed, or endorsed by the original book's author or publisher.

Table of Contents

Overview 4

Important People 6

Key Takeaways..7

Analysis 10

Key Takeaway 1 10

Key Takeaway 2 12

Key Takeaway 3 14

Key Takeaway 4 16

Key Takeaway 5 18

Key Takeaway 6 20

Key Takeaway 7 22

Key Takeaway 8 24

Author's Style 26

Author's Perspective 27

Instaread on The Advantage by Patrick Lencioni

Overview

The Advantage: Why Organizational Health Trumps Everything Else in Business by Patrick Lencioni is a practical guide to organizational health. Organizational health is a characteristic of many successful businesses and organizations. Leaders can adopt organizational health strategies to transform their own operations and company culture in order to see the same successes that many other healthy organizations do. Through analysis, case studies, and applicable step-by-step explanations, executives and leadership teams can uncover where their own organizational health is lacking and how to improve upon it.

The Advantage divides organizational health into four correlating disciplines: building a cohesive leadership team, creating clarity, overcommunicating clarity, and reinforcing clarity. These disciplines build on each other to create a competitive advantage over businesses and organizations that do not take the time to address problems that they might overcome through better organizational health. Comprehension and application of the four disciplines of organizational health can lead to improvements in various aspects of a business, from strategy and finance to marketing and technology. While being a smart business with deep knowledge of the industry is important, being a healthy business can enable a business to be even smarter. An unhealthy organization can be costly not just to company culture, morale, and operations; it can be financially costly, as well.

A more cohesive leadership team, for example, is open, honest, and allows for vulnerability among members of the team. This leads to constructive conflict and better decision-making and top-down communication with other employees. Creating, overcommunicating, and reinforcing clarity ensures the alignment of a leadership team with the rest of the business. This means better communication, strategy, productivity, and work ethic. With these disciplines in mind, meetings become a vital tool for organizational health.

Important People

Patrick Lencioni: Lencioni is the author of the book and has been a business consultant for twenty years, specializing in organizational health. He writes and speaks about these business principles while assisting businesses through his own consultancy firm.

Key Takeaways

1. Organizational health is a crucial factor in the success of a business or organization, as it ensures a competitive advantage over others.

2. Organizational health offers businesses and organizations a competitive advantage mainly because many other leadership teams ignore its value.

3. While businesses and organizations spend a lot of time on organizational intelligence, they must also be healthy. A healthier business is a smarter business, and the two qualities thus combine to achieve greater success.

4. A cohesive leadership team is essential for ensuring that a business or organization remains competitive against its competition and able to achieve the level of success it is pursuing. Without cohesion, leadership may not be setting a good example for the rest of the employees, and leaders may not make optimal business decisions.

5. If a leadership team understands the answers to six questions about its communicational clarity and acts to implement strategies to optimize it, then it has already taken the most important step needed to secure a competitive advantage through organizational health.

6. Leadership teams must not simply communicate but must *overcommunicate* the messages and principles of their organization. Despite some leaders' hesitance to overcommunicate their messages, it is often necessary to ensure that they are heard, believed, and followed throughout the organization.

7. To set an example for employees, clarity and overcommunication have to be supplemented by reinforced messages that are embedded into the foundation of the business and into every decision that leadership makes.

8. After determining the best practices of the four disciplines of organizational health, meetings become a critical venue for implementing those practices.

Thank you for purchasing this Instaread book

Download the Instaread mobile app to get unlimited text & audio summaries of bestselling books.

Visit Instaread.co to learn more.

Instaread on The Advantage by Patrick Lencioni

Analysis

Key Takeaway 1

Organizational health is a crucial factor in the success of a business or organization, as it ensures a competitive advantage over others.

Analysis

While some business leaders believe that aspects of business such as strategy, finance, or marketing are the keys to success, organizational health may play a much larger role. Organizational health can contribute to the successes of those other aspects of business by providing them with clearer context and arming them with tools for overcoming obstacles. Most important among these tools is better communication. By pursuing the improvement of organizational health, businesses and organizations gain a competitive advantage that enables them to increase efficiency and efficacy of operations while also benefitting company culture and morale.

Achieving a competitive advantage is a top priority for many businesses and organizations of all sizes, especially in industries where the market is saturated with competitors, such as technology, health care, or digital communications. Hoping to boost company morale and productivity, a digital communications firm may have tried improving assorted employee perks and on-site benefits, such as daily catered lunch or a pool table in the break room. However, leaders might grow frustrated if morale and productivity remain low because employees view these added perks as the leadership's attempt to shirk responsibility for deeper problems. Although a digital communications firm, this company's internal communication, particularly between the leadership and employees, might be strained. Employees may feel that memos from management are convoluted with mixed messages, while management believes its employees are not dedicated to their jobs. These are signs of an unhealthy organization that needs to rethink the foundational behaviors and thought processes that regulate its daily procedures and decisions.

Key Takeaway 2

Organizational health offers businesses and organizations a competitive advantage mainly because many other leadership teams ignore its value.

Analysis

Despite the advantages of doing so, many businesses do not take advantage of principles for achieving organizational health. Three particular biases tend to prevent businesses and organizations from embracing the strategies behind improving organizational health, despite the benefits. A sophistication bias occurs when leaders believe organizational health is not going to make a significant difference or underestimate its importance because the changes are so simple, straightforward, and obvious. With the adrenaline bias, leaders are so focused on all of the activity going on in their company that they do not stop to address the types of issues that can make an organization unhealthy and dysfunctional. The quantification bias means leaders have a hard time accepting organizational health because the concept is difficult, if not impossible, to quantify with any hard metrics, such as return on investment.

An executive at a health care company, the chief of finance, may be hesitant to embrace organizational health methods because he feels that his multi-billion dollar company needs something more substantial than daily, five-minute check-in meetings, or more vulnerability and productive conflict among leadership. He believes that a company as large as his would require a more complex strategy to improve performance — one less based on the emotions of the group, which he feels he cannot measure adequately. He is afraid he would not be able to prove how those changes might generate higher sales and show return on investment to the company's shareholders. These patterns of thinking exemplify the sophistication bias and quantification bias.

However, another executive, the chief of operations, does believe that operational health initiatives could improve company performance. She explains to the CFO that she has seen how daily check-in meetings improve regular communication among the leadership teams at rival companies. She attempts to dispel the chief of finance's sophistication bias by explaining how these check-in meetings kept another company on track with internal projects better than before the meetings were instituted. This ended up saving the company time and money: they seldom needed to backtrack or hold long meetings to clear up confusion among the different leaders. Thinking back to his own company's long meetings and how wasteful he often finds them, the chief of finance rethinks his doubts.

Key Takeaway 3

While businesses and organizations spend a lot of time on organizational intelligence, they must also be healthy. A healthier business is a smarter business, and the two qualities thus combine to achieve greater success.

Analysis

Being a smart business is certainly important. Understanding a business's industry and aspects of operations such as marketing and technology is crucial to business success. Knowledge about these aspects of a business can be described as decision science. At the same time, being a smart business high in organizational intelligence is only part of what makes a business successful. Organizational health can improve upon organizational intelligence when implemented correctly.

For example, imagine a Silicon Valley tech startup has recruited an intelligent leadership team made up of the top talent in their respective fields. Members of the team have dedicated countless hours to researching their industry, their target audience, market forecasts, and their competitors' products and business models. Armed with this business knowledge, the startup feels prepared to launch their new product, a new mobile payment app, which the leadership team believes could upend the mobile payments industry. However, the leaders disagree on how to interpret the business intelligence they have, and cannot reach decisions required for a clear launch strategy. This has postponed their product's launch date on several occasions, leaving employees confused and frustrated. Since the startup first began working on its product and gathering its business intelligence, two other competing companies have launched similar products, which has contributed to the startup's own product launch problems.

While having a smart business will be important to this startup's success, the startup may never be able to attain that success because the organization is so unhealthy that its leaders cannot make the timely decisions needed to actually launch the product.

Instaread on The Advantage by Patrick Lencioni

Key Takeaway 4

A cohesive leadership team is essential for ensuring that a business or organization remains competitive against its competition and able to achieve the level of success it is pursuing. Without cohesion, leadership may not be setting a good example for the rest of the employees, and leaders may not make optimal business decisions.

Analysis

The members of a cohesive leadership team are open and honest, vulnerable, and trusting. They enter into constructive conflicts, correct individual behaviors that are not aligned with the business, and concentrate on the good of the entire business rather than just themselves or their department. A cohesive leadership team believes in the collective success of the business even when sacrifices have to be made, whether this means giving up resources to another department or making sacrifices of time or emotion doing things that may be outside their realm of responsibility. Without this type of cohesive and unified leadership, a business or organization does not have a good chance of achieving a high level of organizational health.

For example, imagine that the upper management of a food manufacturing company has had problems aligning itself as a team. The chief marketing officer focuses only on how the budget might affect his present and future campaigns, while the chief of innovation lobbies only for more money for his research and development efforts. The chief finance officer is not willing to spread much of the budget around due to perceived financial risks near the end of the fiscal quarter, but marketing and research and development could contribute to top-line growth and innovation for the company. This leadership team does not share a vision for how to allocate resources. As a result, members of individual departments have difficulty cooperating with each other on interdepartmental projects, as employees tend to emulate the divisive nature the company's leadership has taken on. This has meant lackluster results across the board for the past few quarters, which is why the chief finance officer is hesitant to offer more funds to these projects. Now a disagreement has become a cyclical process leading the company on a downward trajectory.

If the leadership team were more cohesive, the different department heads would be able to work together, find ways to compromise about whatever limited funds might be available, and make decisions that are more beneficial to the company's overall success. If he understands the reasons why more investment in marketing and innovation could be better for the overall company's future, rather than limit his concern to the way a budget shortfall might look to the company's board members, the chief of finance might allocate more resources to those departments. Without this compromise, collective understanding, and overall cohesion, miscommunication and conflict can lead to uninformed and uninspired decisions that lead to stagnation. Seeing the leadership team work together cohesively could inspire the employees within each department to work together better, as well.

Key Takeaway 5

If a leadership team understands the answers to six questions about its communicational clarity and acts to implement strategies to optimize it, then it has already taken the most important step needed to secure a competitive advantage through organizational health.

Analysis

Businesses and organizations can ask themselves six questions to clarify different aspects of their business, and the answers to those questions will go on to mold every communication and decision they make. First is to find the organization's core purpose or the reason why the business exists. Next, businesses must decide what types of behaviors are tolerated in their organization. Third, organizations should then determine what it is they do by asking what specific tasks they perform to support their core purpose. Fourth, the leadership team must design a strategy for how they plan to succeed at what they do and why they are doing it. With a clear strategy in mind, they may then determine the answer to the fifth question: deciding what is most important at their present moment and what will have the most immediate and tangible impact. This is their thematic goal. The last step is to determine responsibilities and assign them appropriately to different parts of the leadership team, departments, and other employees.

Without knowing the basics of who they are, what they do, and why they do it, organizations can easily lose track of their goals. A technology startup may begin with the intention of creating a social platform to help college students communicate for group projects and research. The startup's purpose is to help these students collaborate more effectively, create better group work, and earn higher grades. The startup's core values and behaviors are high respect for education and dedication to improving the way students interact. The startup outlines its overall and daily tasks that support that purpose, then creates their strategy and determines what is most important at that moment, which in the beginning is to work out the kinks in the platform through careful attention to coding and programming. However, as team members work with test groups of students, they realize that what many of these students actually need is not a communication platform but rather an actual collaborative online work station. If this discovery is clearly communicated back to the leadership team, the organization's leadership will then realize this type of product would serve the startup's purpose even better. Since such a product will also be more useful to their core audience, it may even make the company more financially successful.

Key Takeaway 6

Leadership teams must not simply communicate but must overcommunicate the messages and principles of their organization. Despite some leaders' hesitance to overcommunicate their messages, it is often necessary to ensure that they are heard, believed, and followed throughout the organization.

Analysis

Sometimes people are skeptical about what management tells them until leadership continues to convey that message consistently over time. Leadership teams need to do more than just send one email to employees when they explain business decisions or other changes to the organization. It will take not just repeated communication but also communications across multiple channels and even from multiple people to ensure that employees receive and understand the message they are delivered. Sometimes leaders are hesitant to overcommunicate to their employees because they find it inefficient and a waste of time for both leaders and employees. Others are worried employees might be insulted by hearing the same message over and over again. Regardless, even many employees themselves understand the need for repetition of messages from leadership, particularly when it comes to consistency over time.

While a leadership team might be enthusiastic about a business decision guiding the direction they are taking the company, the rest of the company may not understand what is happening at first. Leadership may send out a memo or hold a quick meeting to brief employees on what is happening or what will happen in the future, but those employees still may not understand the message the leadership team is trying to communicate.

For example, if a company is merging with another, employees may start to worry about their job security. If the leadership team is not careful to overcommunicate what is happening or might happen to their employees, those employees may start making assumptions or drawing their own conclusions about what will happen next, which could erode morale and productivity. Instead, the leadership team can make the merger and its implications clearly understood by communicating through various channels about what the merger is, why it is happening, and what it means for employees. If the merger requires layoffs, the leadership team could take the opportunity to explain the details surrounding those layoffs to the affected employees and support their efforts to find new employment. If layoffs are not happening, stating that clearly and repeatedly from the outset means that employees would be less likely to spread false information at the water cooler. Rumors cause problems for managers trying to keep their employees on task.

When leaders worry that repeating these messages could be a waste of time, what they should remember is the amount of time that could be wasted having to backtrack or correct misinformation that was spread among employees because the messages were not clear and consistent to begin with. An investment of time and energy repeating messages and maintaining clarity from the outset can save time, energy, and even money later down the line.

Instaread on The Advantage by Patrick Lencioni

Key Takeaway 7

To set an example for employees, clarity and overcommunication have to be supplemented by reinforced messages that are embedded into the foundation of the business and into every decision that leadership makes.

Analysis

Leadership teams must go beyond crafting a clear message and overcommunicating the message to employees. Leaders must also weave those messages into the very fabric of the business and integrate the business's values and principles into the structure of operations and the way leadership makes business decisions. This involves creating human systems that reinforce clarity, which may include recruiting and hiring, orientation, performance management, compensation and rewards, recognition, and firing. By driving messages home not just through written and verbal communication but through reinforcements in structure and decision-making, leaders can deliver better clarity to employees, which can improve morale, productivity, and company culture.

Without reinforcement, messages from leadership can seem hollow or even dishonest. If leadership says one thing, or repeats that same message, but does not follow through when it comes time to practice what they said in their message, employees will not believe those messages or apply them to their jobs. For example, if management begins communicating cutbacks in spending for the business as a whole, leadership should also reinforce the message by cutting back some of their own spending, such as business travel or daily lunch served at the office. If employees see their own budgets being cut while leadership continues to spend money on things that are not necessities for the business and its operations, it sends mixed messages and clouds the clarity that the business needs for optimal organizational health.

Integrating the business's values into the structure of human systems can better ensure fairness and increase morale among employees. If one employee is fired for a certain negative or damaging behavior, but another employee is not because his sales numbers were higher, this sends mixed messages about what is acceptable behavior for employees. Some may find the scenario to be unfair and may spread rumors or even act out against management or the person who was not fired. Morale and productivity might then fall among other employees. To reinforce the message that a particular negative behavior might damage the business and will therefore not be tolerated, both employees must be fired. This builds that message into the structure of the business by reinforcing what leadership deems to be acceptable ways for employees to behave.

Key Takeaway 8

After determining the best practices of the four disciplines of organizational health, meetings become a critical venue for implementing those practices.

Analysis

Meetings are one of the most common communication tools that businesses and organizations use, but too often meetings are ineffective because they are disorganized or poorly conducted. Sometimes employees and management may even dread their regular meetings. While bad meetings can be detrimental to organizational health, good meetings can be the building blocks for establishing better clarity and communication. Businesses need to structure a plan for what types of meetings they hold, when those meetings will take place, and how they will be conducted. Different types of meetings are effective for achieving different results: brief, individual daily check-ins help keep everyone on track with projects, while weekly tactical staff meetings are better for discussing how the business is running as a whole.

Meetings should ultimately become something that team members and employees look forward to: a forum for discussing ideas and solving problems, rather than a begrudged weekly drain of an hour or two of worktime. When implemented properly, meetings can be some of the most productive times of day. Sending employees clear messages about the purpose and structure of meetings, especially at the beginning of their implementation, is just as important as the messages shared at the meetings. This will prevent an ad hoc topical meeting from being bogged down by small details that should be discussed at daily check-ins.

Author's Style

Patrick Lencioni takes a practical approach to the concept of organizational health. Instead of reporting on statistics that might interest the business leaders who read this book, the author sticks to a more qualitative approach. In place of hard data, he uses concrete examples and observations drawn from his many years as a consultant. The author weaves both real and fictional examples of strategies for achieving organizational health into the conceptual explanations and practical steps outlined in the text. Stories and case studies demonstrate the successful application of certain abstract concepts. Other times, the stories illustrate how a company failed or experienced problems because it did not institute or maintain its organizational health as prescribed by the concept discussed in that section.

In each chapter, the author provides a comprehensive overview of a particular model, strategy, or other overarching theme. He then defines the chapter's subtopics, provides a concrete example of each concept, and offers a step-by-step approach that businesses can use to apply the discipline or strategy to their own operations. Throughout the book, Lencioni also references his previous books, some of which are fictional accounts that exemplify topics he illustrates in this book. These fictional scenarios and their accompanying analysis supplement the practical information the author delivers in each chapter.

Author's Perspective

Patrick Lencioni has written several fiction and non-fiction books about aspects of organizational health and related business topics. Lencioni has been a business consultant for twenty years. He started out working for a management consulting firm, followed by a stint in corporate America, where he consulted with businesses on matters of organizational health in a more theoretical way. Neither of these jobs was as fulfilling to Lencioni as taking a more hands-on approach to helping businesses succeed. Lencioni then founded his own firm and began consulting and speaking about the practical nature of organizational health and how businesses can apply various strategies for achieving it, including those outlined in this book.

~~~~ **END OF INSTAREAD** ~~~~

Instaread on The Advantage by Patrick Lencioni

Thank you for purchasing this Instaread book

**Download the Instaread mobile app to get
unlimited text & audio summaries
of bestselling books.**

Visit Instaread.co
to learn more.

Lightning Source UK Ltd.
Milton Keynes UK
UKHW022334270819
348691UK00013B/3301/P